6/29/17

THE CHARMER

– Poems –

Jack Lynch

Jimmy —
I hope you enjoy
the poems
Jack

R&Q Press

THE CHARMER
Jack Lynch
R&Q Press, Inc.

Copyright © 2017 by Reed and Quill Press

No part of this publication may be reproduced or transmitted in any fashion including being stored or moved into any retrieval system, transmitted by any means or form including electronic, photocopying, digital, recording, mechanical, or any other copying method without prior written permission of this book's publisher and copyright owner.

Published by Reed & Quill Press, Inc.
107-13 29th Avenue
Flushing, New York 11358
RnQPress@aol.com

ISBN: 978-0-9894166-0-3
Printed in the United States of America
All rights reserved.

for the poets of the world

CONTENTS

SHARING / 9

SAILING FROM DUBROVNIK / 10

UNDER THE HOUSE / 11

PIANO CONCERT IN NORWAY / 12

DIANA AND THE MOON / 13

WHERE'S WALLY? / 14

JAMES JOYCE / 15

ROSIE / 16

THE HOARDER / 17

SHAKING THINGS UP / 19

FOLLOWING RIMBAUD / 20

THE VAGABOND / 21

TIMMY THE MOPE / 22

THE SAMBA / 23

SHE LOVES HER MUSIC / 24

MRS. ROCCO / 25

A GOOD NEIGHBOR IS HARD TO FIND / 26

PAM / 27

AUNT BLANCHE / 28

THE SWEDE / 29

WHY? / 30

FATHER TO SON / 31

EDVARD MUNCH / 32

WATERFRONT BAR IN BARBADOS / 33

SUBLET, ANYONE? / 35

THE RACE / 37

ASTORIA / 38

THE CITY / 39

AUNTIE JANE'S RENTAL / 40

THE STAGE / 41

THE DESERT / 42

RAIN / 43

IN THE NAVY / 44

RETURNING HOME / 45

MAGNOLIA / 46

THE AFFAIR / 47

FROM HER POINT OF VIEW / 48

A CHANGE OF PLANS / 49

TABLES GET TURNED / 51

THE ONE NOT THERE / 52

JUST LAST NIGHT / 53

MORE THAN A MARGARITA / 54

INTO THE NIGHT / 55

RELUCTANCE / 56

COYOTES / 57

THE SQUIRREL IN CENTRAL PARK / 58

THE SEAGULL / 59

SERPENTS AND TENTACLES / 61

CHOICES / 63

THE LIGHT OF DAY / 64

WRITING POETRY ON NEW PAPER / 66

SURF NOT TURF / 67

THE THIRD VOLCANO / 68

JUST A WORLD WITHOUT WORDS / 69

TWO POETS IN THE FOG / 70

UNTIL / 71

THREE WOMEN / 72

IN THE MEMORY OF RABINDRANATH TAGORE / 73

KIRSTEN / 74

HOVERING / 75

HOODIE / 76

MOHONK / 77

COME TO ME / 78

THE TRAIN STATION / 79

THE POSTCARD / 80

THE CHARMER / 81

DARK CITY IN THE SAND / 82

TIBIDABO IN BARCELONA / 83

ACKNOWLEDGMENT / 84

SHARING

A boxer in a hurry
runs through Central Park

. . . a lady assassin
hides in the dark.

. . . a Pakistani dentist

. . . and a ravishing queen

all together
use the X-ray machine.

Isn't it nice
so many different people
using the same device.

SAILING FROM DUBROVNIK

This is no city
for young men
who flee to the sea
taking the little they have.

Images of wars:
bullet holes in doors and trees,
chunks of broken walls.

There's no such thing as music;
no one dares to sing,
no desire to look at places
ruined by fire.
Tangled in sadness
they leave and grieve
for a broken city.

UNDER THE HOUSE

Secrets
hidden
in that cellar,
under the house.
Who would sleep
in that dark, dank place?
Bottles, jars, empty cans
everywhere.
One small dirty
window by the boiler
creating a dingy light.
The odor of spilled whiskey
and damp mold
overwhelms.
Years of clammy grime and filth
stops entry.
No one wants to go down there but me.
Shadows become ghosts. You could hide
a dead life down there.
Maybe one day,
I'll disappear
under
the house.

PIANO CONCERT IN NORWAY

Knowing this music,
we dressed with care.
The concert was held
in Edvard Grieg's house.
My wife put on her finest silk stockings,
and an old Norwegian brooch,
along with her favorite black dress.
Suddenly, out of nowhere
a money argument surfaced;
as we got into the car,
torrents of rain began.
We arrived and took our seats
in the intimate hall.
It poured through most of the concert.
Lightning and thunder added to the ambiance.
I was swept away in a kind of joy,
forgetting myself as I joined
the music. I was in a different world.
I glanced at my wife, tears in her eyes.
We embraced.

DIANA AND THE MOON

Alone.
    Alone
        in the kitchen.
            Trapped by dishes and pots...
    she had to go
but where?
There, the hidden door;
she moves quickly on the
    waxed floor.
        Suddenly, fresh air...her face, pale
            under the full moon
        Finally free, she runs
    through the pine trees which
open
to a lake and resort.
    Catching her breath, she slowly moves to the music.
        Her bright blue eyes fall upon
            a dancer and his eyes
        fall upon her.
    He approaches her
and they dance to the tango.
Images of the moon
    and pines swirl around them;
        they laugh with joy
            and passion.

WHERE'S WALLY?

Where's Wally, the alcoholic
    who changed wives without divorce?
Was he aware? Did he care?
    And what happened to Rose,
stagestruck Rose, always on her toes?
    Sulking, waiting for her big break?
Then there was Franz who loved to dance
    and did he end up in France?
Is mad Mimi around
    who loved her coke?
Is she still afloat and always broke?
    I looked for Sally, wild Sally who loved
her booze, only to find her in an
    alley, singing the blues.
Where's tough Mel, the boxer
    who went down at the bell
losing his fight in the final round?
    GUESS WHAT?
They are all like me, waiting,
    waiting to be somebody…

JAMES JOYCE

It begins on the banks of the River Liffey,
in Dublin where Joyce was bred (and buttered):
    the alcoholic father,
the suffering mother and
    Nora Barnacle, his wife and muse.
"Barnacle by name, barnacle by nature."
    She'd stick with him through thick and thin.
He flees sweet Ireland to Paris, Trieste,
    and Zurich but can never forget his
Dublin entangled forever
    in music and dreams.
He would flee Nora, too, once in a while
    sneaking out to get a bottle of wine
or to reread a section
    of Molly Bloom's reverie.
The delicate tapestry
    of his life and work
are left for us to enjoy.

ROSIE

I'm in my T-shirt and shorts
dressed for summer days,
but it's very cold this morning.
How did this happen?
I'm out of season, for no reason.

I'm eating eggs at the diner
Where I always eat pancakes.
Rosie, the waitress, shakes her head.
I'm smiling instead of
my usual frowning.

I dreamed of kissing Rosie last night.
I never have dreams;
Something strange is going on,
some kind of transformation.
Eureka! I'm in love with Rosie!

THE HOARDER

He was withdrawn
and getting paler every day;
the papers were closing in on him.
Where were his taxes?
He began digging through the stacks against the wall.
He was warned that one day this would happen.
He went to get his ladder
in the closet.
It was covered by papers and garbage bags.
There wasn't room for clothes in this place;
there were only books and vacuum cleaners.
Why did he need seven vacuum cleaners?
Finally, he was able to get the ladder out
to climb it to the top box
labeled important papers.
From his high perch
he was able to view his messy kingdom.
His apartment was a graveyard without stones.
He grabbed the top box
but almost fell with it,
then slowly moved down the ladder.
Reaching the floor, he opened his container
only to find his important papers were
old comic books. Where were his taxes?
The bell rang. He hated people bothering

him when he was trying to find something important.

It was his brother Harvey
who began lecturing him: "Look at this place.
It's a fire hazard. You're a hoarder. There's something
wrong with you. Can't you try to help yourself?"

"My taxes must be here somewhere," he answered.

SHAKING THINGS UP

It was a dive bar in Brooklyn;
    they called it Rocco's.
He loved working there;
    pouring wine and beer all day never
bothered him.
    He doled out advice
when people asked,
    drawing the line on politics.
Sharing stories was what he remembered.
    He's seventy-five years old now,
lost his wife a year ago;
    he fell in love with her
at first sight:
    he a bartender,
she a waitress
    across the avenue.
He went back working
    at the old dinky bar.
It wasn't the same though.
    Everyone either died or left.
"I've got to shake things up around here,"
    he tells everyone,
"and make things like it used to be!"

FOLLOWING RIMBAUD

There is a place in Ireland in the north
 far away; it's peaceful there today.
Once it was filled with hatred fear, dark nights and black skies.
Lies still appear, and curses too.
A poet was born under the railway arches;
people in their homes barred their windows;
soldiers were in the street standing guard.
For many years he lived surrounded by the troubles.
He was hardly aware his words had power.
Every lyric he created was rewarded with drink.
His eyes began to fail but visions flooded his mind.
Verse grew special to his ear, to hell with all else.
Let's celebrate with whiskey, that's all he wanted to hear.

THE VAGABOND

Some days I just drift
        like a boat upon a
                velvet river;
everything I plan. . .
        just fades away.

So I give myself
        to the undercurrents
before touching the water's
edge. . .
        my new home.

TIMMY THE MOPE

when we were kids
   he used to sneak us into the movies.
      we knew where to go.
         the narrow alleyway that led to the door
        you could always find him there
      or else on the corner selling papers
   and taking bets on the nags.
he would swing himself with his crutches,
his right leg a stump instead of a leg.
   his bald head and hunchback completed
the picture. When we were older we'd
      give him some food, or money, or a bottle.
     and he'd give us some tips on the horses.
    they never came in. . .it didn't matter.
   he had some great stories, that Timmy.
i really miss him.

THE SAMBA

She dances,
samba-addicted:
music warms her
and speaks to us.

She unpins her hair
and lets it fly;
there is a look of rapture
on her face.

She's Brazilian;
dancing makes her forget,
the good, the bad,
and the ugly.

Her hips sway
to the beat
moving faster and faster;
everyone shouts for more.

SHE LOVES HER MUSIC

She self-medicates:
drinks copious amounts of alcohol
and abuses pills
without prescription.
Such combinations
bring about altered states.

When you're a punk rocker
with an edgy voice,
you live in
Rockaway Beach, Queens, New York.
She loves playing all night;
it's always the morning that hurts like hell.
Despair takes over.
She stops cold turkey.
Suddenly, three people she loved are dead:
her son, her husband, and father.
She wants to kill herself. She survives.
A year later, she begins to write her story,
too difficult and never finished.
So she jumps back into her punk rock band.
The drugs are still there
everywhere.

MRS. ROCCO

Renters come and go
thinking of Mrs. Rocco, their landlady;
so let us go now,
you and I,
and make a visit
to a four-story apartment house.

She rules the roost
that Mrs. Rocco,
unlocking renters' rooms
when she sees fit.
This woman knows everything.
She knows when they are quiet
and jumps when they move.
She knows if they take drugs
or if they drink too much. Last week she saw a puta
climbing into Pedro's window on the first floor.
Yes, without her tenants, she would die.
They are her life; she also likes to see what they're eating,
rummaging through the garbage cans each morning.
Like a lover, she must know all.

A GOOD NEIGHBOR IS HARD TO FIND

Tina opens her door; she lets him in.
They sit at the table
and talk about things:
laughing at unfulfilled dreams.
Tina cooks his favorite soup
and gives him a baked potato.
It seems like they get along well.
When the downstairs bell rings he leaves.
The next day they have a meal
and a few drinks. He understands her problems:
lack of money, loss of passion.
They move to the next step.
A month later, he leaves
to find another good neighbor.
The baked potatoes just don't taste the same.
The soup is not so good,
so he leaves her and looks for a new neighbor.
He can't find one; hungry, he
returns to Tina's floor only to find
Jim Murphy from upstairs
knocking, knocking at her door.

PAM

They captured her picture
...front page in the local paper.
When the news reached the old guys at the lunch counter,
they were shocked. She was like a second wife.
"The Stop Inn Diner would never be the same," said Sam.
After fourteen years of waitressing Pam was going on the lam.
"How could she do this?" was the cry. You could hear
each man sigh. She poured their first coffee in the morning,
said such tender things like,
"Hi, honey—coffee?"
"How about a bagel? Eggs, sunnyside up?"
"Over easy? Poached? Any meat?"
"Bacon, ham, or sausage? Say, how you been?"
"I missed you yesterday. It's good to see yah."
She was the girl of their dreams... a little chunky maybe, and she oughta do
something with that hair, always with the ponytail, but she's young, that's
the main thing. A peach of a girl. She sets down the eggs, gives Conroy's hand
a pat and the tremor stops—the old goat is healed in a second. She pours
coffee for Butch, her hand brushes against his and he trembles. He reaches for
her and she's gone. Her reply? "This job is like being married to my husband,
so I'm leaving , killing two birds with one stone:
husband and job... goodbye you all."

AUNT BLANCHE

My lovely aunt
whose name is Blanche
sits by her window,
brushing her hair.
How calmly she watches
one lonely branch
while thinking of her past.

Sometimes, stormy nights
obscure the tree;
she thinks of how
her life could be.

Her storytelling
is not well designed
leaving friends
with nothing kind,
nothing kind to say.
My lovely aunt
sits by her window
brushing her hair.

THE SWEDE

Lennart Larsson, the Swedish boxer,
lives in my building.
He is well liked. His wife not so much.
When I was young he taught
me how to box and showed
me framed pictures of his
knockouts.
His wife is a very good cook
known for her exotic sauces,
always placing the hot red pepper
sauce on the table with the greatest of care.
Lennart loved her homemade pepper sauce.

One day Lennart's wife ran away with the
plumber; my father and I went
to visit him to console him.
We found him in tears but
after a few shots of whiskey we
started to laugh. You see, he wasn't
crying for his wife; he was crying for
the pepper sauce she put deep into her suitcase!

WHY?

These days I see
my father only in dreams.
His face shows
a kindness it never had.
All his plans
were for me, his son.
He even told me
he loved me,
and that I should come home.
Maybe for Christmas, I told him.
Then it became Easter.
His birthday; my birthday.
Always something.

A few days ago he died.
The neighbors said he was a good man.
My father was a drunk and a drug dealer.
He was always looking for a good time.
He sought out women and made my mother very unhappy.
Why would I have gone home?
To bury myself?

FATHER TO SON

A light is on
in the back room
of my old man's store.
I enter and watch him
working on his beloved watches.
We are silent;
he has a loupe in his eye.
After making a delicate movement
to a small wheel,
he looks up at me...his eyes questioning,
why are you here?
I say nothing...
Not knowing
what to do...
I leave.

        My son enters the room.
        He sees me fixing a watch under the lamp light.
        He watches and doesn't say a word;
        he leaves with a nod.
        It's not what I needed.
        A hug would have been better.
        Maybe...
        tomorrow.

EDVARD MUNCH

Women on the bridge
do not stare
at dark water;
after all,
this is Prague;
do not disturb them.
They meet to talk.
They just nod
in sunlight and
compliment one another.
Nothing matters
except their talk.
Men walk around
their little circle and
look at them with questioning eyes.
Why do they spend
so much time on the bridge?
Compliments turn into criticism.
The sunny day turns
cloudy; suddenly, jealousy
raises its ugly head.
They arrange to meet another day.

WATERFRONT BAR IN BARBADOS

    It's just a waterfront
bar in Barbados
    around sunset
where I'm bogged down
    by pressures and stress.
Ships are docking;
    cargoes are emptying.

    They come from the ends
of the earth
    tinged with reflections
of light blue skies.
    There's a sharp lingering scent
of unknown lands
    and endless journeys.

    I noticed the waitress
with her dragonfly
    earrings
and red lips
    looking at us,
sitting there
    not talking.
Your eyes that once
dived into mine

    without fear
catching my every thought,
    catching my every dream,
now look away,
    so we drink to forget.

    The sailors talk
of women and love;
    we talk about mistakes.
We need mirrors
    to tell us who we are.
I break into pieces;
    I've lost you.

    We only had one drink;
the meal never came.
    There was never anyone
but you.
    The table is between us,
and we leave separately.
    There is nothing else to say.

SUBLET, ANYONE?

    He needed to be alone,
so he sublet an apartment
    from a young woman
in Brooklyn Heights.
    It was cozy, a leather
couch, an easy chair,
    a soft mattress,
a full fridge, and
    foghorns on misty nights.
The first few days
    he was bumping into things,
immersed in another's life:
    her features looking at him
from pictures scattered everywhere:
    Looks of joy, regrets, apologies.
Secret things in the closets,
    that he dared not approach,
places shuttering with lives of
    their own.
The impressions of her were
    everywhere: the chair,
the desk, the narrow bed,
    even the boxes that were
pushed against the walls with
    her letters, papers, memories.

He wanted to take a peek,
    but he did not dare.
After the first month,
    she began to drop by
to take some things away:
    some books one day,
one box another time,
    a small painting one afternoon.
He would share a coffee, or
    a glass of wine.
Then one night she stayed over
    and he was swept away
taking him into another world.
    Slowly she started moving things back.
More boxes were brought in.
    A new bed too and
she was cooking meals.
    Then he knew…
the sublet was over.

THE RACE

I'm in New York at Belmont Race Track;
I need to be here to get lost in the crowd,
to be alone; I don't want to talk.
I walk toward the track entrance.
It's a clear day. Some stocky guy joins me;
he starts asking me who I like.
The track is giving away free T-shirts,
so I ditch him to get one.
I go to check out the horses; I'm prepared.
I watch
horses and jocks
come out for the post parade.
The man to my right calls me Mac and tells me he does
okay with horses; it's only with women that he loses.
Now it's time bet: twenty to win on the four horse
and forty to win on the five horse.
The horses are loaded into the gate—they're off!
They break in a spill of color, taking on the first turn,
fighting for position. There's still a chance for everybody.
They circle the last turn and come down the stretch.
The favorite gives way. My number 4 horse comes on rapidly,
passing the favorite.
He comes in a rush, pounding and driving.
It's exciting;
I forget everything.
I'm a winner—pure joy.

ASTORIA

Bare boards creak in the hallway.
My brother and I pause to look at
two globed hall lights flickering on and off.
All day, it seemed, we travelled on the subway;
first stop was the funeral home. The names we knew but not the faces.
Something like a family album. We saw our cousins,
Lou and Jeannie at their apartment. They showed us the guest room
with two single beds. The springs were popping up all over the place,
and the sheets looked slept in. How would we ever sleep?
Our cousins lost their mother,
and we worried if the sheets were clean.

They took us all over Astoria, to escape the apartment;
they told us stories about their mother, our mother's sister.
They never told us what they were feeling.

Last year, our mother died and they came over to stay with us.
We didn't tell them what we were feeling either.
We took them all over Bay Ridge and Sunset Park.
We were family,
a real family.

THE CITY

You said you would go to another land,
to another sea, a better place than here,
but yet the city follows you wherever
you go. In your mind you roam
the same streets, discover
the same neighborhoods,
always arriving in a city.
Do not hope for any other; it is
in your blood and your body.
It will never leave you.

AUNTIE JANE'S RENTAL

Delia loves the summertime in the Rockaways;
her Auntie Jane has a rental
right by the water.
Delia always sleeps in the room
with the iron bed
and fading blue bedspread.
From the bed she can see herself
in the Coney Island mirror,
always making her look good:
seventeen instead of sixteen.
She loves the armoire with
all its scratches and stains.
It reminds her of a place
in a children's book
she used to read.
The breeze stirs the flimsy curtains;
she turns to the wall where
the calendar hangs,
always showing the wrong month.
Before falling asleep she wonders
if the cute boy from last summer
will be back this year.

THE STAGE

The curtain opens
on a young woman
moving gracefully
across the stage.

Dressed in a blue velvet gown,
she slowly
starts to sing,
her words,
so clear,
so inviting,
her sound,
so powerful
so controlled.
We step
into
her world.
Once there
we never want
to leave;
we never
want it
to end.

THE DESERT

A windless place,
where sand doesn't move,
with temperatures over a hundred,
that's all there is.
Days of frustration
no rain.
Lips parched
and that terrible thirst.

A desert song drifts by,
pictures of sleek vessels
filled with water.
Wild aromas from caravans
soothes.
There is a grove nearby
with sweet shade,
where hidden things are waiting
like the scent of a lemon.

RAIN

A whisper of rain is falling;
my coat is heavy; my boots are wet.

I enter the café; fresh coffee,
and homemade bread welcome me.
Sitting at our table alone, I watch people decompose
in the drizzle; there is only desolation now,
and the sound of wind outside.

Thoughts of you take hold.
Two nights ago you looked in the closet,
and told me there wasn't much wine.
Then you said that
the bed was too narrow.
Maybe I shouldn't have told you I loved you.
You are such a puzzle, always retreating,
so private, so proud.
Streets no longer lead to your house.
Sadly, my words no longer touch you.
Your departure crushes me. Winter has come.
It's getting cold outside.

IN THE NAVY

In the navy
you're taught to dive,
to stay alive
just in case your ship
sinks in the drink.
      In this school
      by the deep pool
      I hear feet
      slip on wet tile;
we move
to a higher platform
near the deep pool.
Our heads throb
with fear.
      I pitch forward.
      I am free, until the water
      hits hard and fast.
      I touch bottom, and
      hurry to survive.
Robert Frost wrote about dying
in fire and ice. Die at sea? Not me.
Put me in the army please.

RETURNING HOME

My father's hand
is stiff and cold
like old leather.
He cannot make
a fist anymore
to hurt…
My mother has
dishwater eyes.
She hurries to hug me,
as she dries her hands.
There are no stars
tonight; there's only a
soft rain falling.
The neighbor's dog
barks; my wife
returns with clementines.
They are soft
like her lips.
Her body
knows the darkness
within me
repeating
the mystery
of life.

MAGNOLIA

"Will you be my magnolia,
take my hand
and love me forever?
When I'm all alone
And a cold wind blows,
will you warm me
with your kisses?
Will you squeeze me tightly
each morning,
as if I were an orange?
And will you serve me
my breakfast in bed?
I loved it
when you shined
my shoes
last Tuesday.
Show me the way,
my sweet magnolia."

"I'll show you the way," she said.
"Forget about it!"

THE AFFAIR

It's very cold out; he leaves
her house early in the morning,
looking around to see if the neighbors
are watching. This warm rosy
woman still has her hands on him,
hands moving
under his coat holding his hips, letting him know
she doesn't want him to leave.
He doesn't want to leave.
He takes a deep breath and then another.
A final kiss and she lets him go.
He walks slowly to his car.
He breaks into a smile
thinking of their night of love.
When he reaches the apartment
he relaxes fully.
He's home.
He begins grinding the beans for coffee.
The doorbell rings.
It's her, his wife with her suitcase.
"It was a wonderful trip, darling,
but I've lost my keys."

FROM HER POINT OF VIEW

When he left her that
very cold morning,
something was different.
The knowledge was
sharp and painful
as he reached
for a fast goodbye.

It started with no space
between them
and then the space grew
and the person she knew
was slowly disappearing.
The part of him she loved
was now an empty space;
only weak gestures remained.
The words he once whispered,
were gone forever.
She wanted him back
into her warm bed.
But she felt like crying.
What do you say when it's over?

A CHANGE OF PLANS

You asked me why.
What could I say?
Friends told me, "Don't stay!
Leave her today!"

Climb away from your shore,
taking the back road from your door;
travel south away from the cold rain,
the dark days, the pain.

I found fun in my new world,
with plenty of sun, blue water
and dazzling clouds…
warm sweet evenings,
until
the sea reflected your eyes,
and the sun reminded me of your hair,
and the laughter sounded like your voice.
Beach, birds, all within reach.

But I returned.
Why? What did I want?
It's that look I can't erase,
even in this dreary space.
Your voice sings in my heart;

it tells me we will never part.
You make me feel alive;
you're the reason I survive.
I'll take your laughter and your fears;
I'll take your joy and your tears.
I want your arms holding me,
your love touching me.
Stranger, lover, friend,
this is not the end.
Pour the wine;
it's all fine.
It's my choice;
I'll never leave again.

TABLES GET TURNED

He had a lover,
named Michelle,
who loved to hover over him.
Then he fell for another…
for the heart changes,
and his changed a lot.
Then Michelle returned,
and again he fell
under her spell.
Sadly her love for him
had changed;
it was not like,
it was.
The sweetness was gone;
it shocked him.
He was lost;
was that what she wanted?

Endless, endless sorrow
was what
she wanted.
She left him,
for good.

THE ONE NOT THERE

Throw away the key
and walk away;
that's what I want
to do today.

There was a time when
I would float down the street,
lost with your hand in mine,
enjoying the waves of your splendor.

We often played in the ocean
like dolphins
watching the clouds
float by.

I remember the music we shared
on warm afternoons.
You had white flowers
in your hair.

I still think of you,
your voice,
your touch,
your scent.

Where could you be?

JUST LAST NIGHT

I didn't expect you
to sit by me
in the blue mist
of twilight
changing
my life, forever.

My surprised eyes
saw your sweet look
and never wavered.
Your face blushed
at my inquiring eyes.
I knew at that moment
I would have a heart
tattooed
with your name
inside
on my arm.

MORE THAN A MARGARITA

He began to loiter by her desk.
It was lunch hour; he was telling her
he could finish work by noon.
He was in his twenties, tall and brash.
One Tuesday he invited her for a liquid lunch.
She liked the idea.
The old-fashioned dark wood bar,
was soothing. Over margaritas
she saw him better. She liked him.
His right hand covered hers and he kissed
her after the second drink.
They met two days later at the same place.
The bartender smiled as he delivered
their third round of drinks; a current
ran down her body when he touched her thigh.
Her appetite got rescheduled: passion for lunch?
The dance with guilt began: she was late getting back.
All resolutions broken:
they were cheating on company time.

INTO THE NIGHT

On the way home
I passed you
in the street;
we saw each other,
but you never
said a word.

I turned around
hoping you'd
turn too,
but
you never
did.

I was
so cold…
so cold
not hearing
your voice so
warm…
so warm.

RELUCTANCE

I'm reluctant
    to let
        the moment
            go,
but it slips
    away
        anyway.
            The heat
of the
    moment
        takes
            a wisp
of your lovely hair
    entwining it
        into
            mine.

COYOTES

A group of us came to this southern Californian place.
We found a strange, derelict house with narrow staircases
that shuddered and creaked. Darkness seeped through the ribs of this old house.
We start a bonfire close to the barn.
We start drinking and singing songs; the branches and logs are burning.
We tell stories. The coyote story surprises us.
Jim tells us coyotes roam in loosely knit packs.
Native Americans in this area believed they took the form
of a man, a trickster of sorts. Suddenly, we hear
an eerie sound. We hear a howling that makes us all shiver.
Where is it coming from? We leave and move
To the porch huddling closer together.
We hear the coyotes increasing their raucous chorus. Drinking is our
only defense as we listen to the ominous sounds. We become uneasy.
A full moon doesn't help. They are coming closer.
We run inside, and
stay up half the night, peeking through the windows.
Then we hear a knock on the door. "Don't answer it," someone says.
"Don't be ridiculous," Jim says and as opens the door.
No one is there. No one tells another story. No one sleeps. We're exhausted.
Years later, we still talk about the trickster who
knocked at the door.

THE SQUIRREL IN CENTRAL PARK

Today I found myself
watching a squirrel
near Turtle Pond.
He was burying
some nuts of sorts.
Seeing me,
he moved his bushy tail
and ran around a tree.
I followed him.
His large brown eyes grew larger,
claws grasped the bark
preparing for a game of hide and seek.
He climbed up the tree
to the other side.
I ran after him with my walnut in hand
and threw it to him.
We became fast friends.
I promised to come back tomorrow
with pecans.

THE SEAGULL
for Jim Kochones

    one day Jim died;
they brought his heart back
    like a tuft of grass
that turns to hay
    and becomes green again.

    so he vowed to change
and try something new.
    With his beloved nurse, Calypso near
he changed his name
    and they flew away to Greece.

    there he married her;
they drank retsina
    and ate grapes;
their skin turned olive
    and the sun gave them children.

    they grew old together;
their children flew away;
    one by one they left
and in time his beloved Calypso
    passed away.
    he returned

  to New York
    to be born again,
looking for a life
   of peace.

   one day he sat
by the sea,
   where a seagull landed
on a railing close by;
    they glanced at one another.

   without past or future
each bathing in the sea breeze,
   feeling the sun,
at that very moment he knew
    what it meant.

SERPENTS AND TENTACLES

Last night
I went to the pier;
I stood alone,
waiting and watching.

Light rain began to fall
as fog covered the river.
Bells and horns
echoed.

I felt lost
thinking of my father.
In the distance
a ship on the lifting tide.

Was it my father's
lost at sea so long ago?
I felt a pull
towards its darkened hull.

I stepped aside in fear
as the huge ship came near.
I heard
my father calling.

Suddenly, he was beside me
leaning over the edge,
staring at the dark water;
there was a wall of silence.

Below the sea,
images of serpents called to me.
Tentacles wrapped my arm
pulling me close.

My father's strong hands
grasped me
and took me back;
once again, I stood alone.

CHOICES

My old lady
told me
Pete had called
while I was out.
Shouting from the other room
I asked, "Is he in Barcelona?"
She didn't know but said
he would call back.
When I came into the kitchen
she said, "I guess he wants to meet
up with you. He always calls
when desperate for money."
"Now, now, he's a good buddy of mine.
Remember we traveled a lot together.
I stayed with you, baby. Didn't I?"
The phone started to ring,
"Don't answer," she said.
I picked up the phone,
"Hi, Pete."

THE LIGHT OF DAY

Two nights ago, I dreamt about
the Banda Islands where nutmeg
thrives. I was attacked
by a gang and left for dead.
Last night I dreamt of Baghdad
surrounded by the enemy
with no place to hide;
I'm dead again.
My mind plays tricks on me
both awake and sleeping.
At night, death
stalks me, but here I am.
I'm here watching
my wife
make breakfast.
Am I a ghost? For a while,
I'm safe at this table
with no mortars,
dust, or heat.
I eat my oatmeal.
I begin tying my shoes.
A car backfires and I flinch.
My wife comes to the table
and hugs me.

My father
would have loved this scene.
Breakfast is over;
my wife makes the bed;
I'm alone at the table.

WRITING POETRY ON NEW PAPER

A gift from a fan…
don't get many of them…
so I have to smile
when one comes my way…
a packet of five hundred sheets of long grain.
Yes, that's what the cover says,
plain white paper.

My fan wants more poems…a good sign. Opening this package
seems sinful…it's luxurious and silky; I long to write on the purity
of these pages. I've been writing on scrap paper all my life,
with print on the other side. Actually, I like the printing on the other side,
a much needed distraction. With my new white paper there will
be no straying. I have to be careful. I must
write without mistakes…no more doodling, no more scribbling
or ink stains. It just doesn't look good.
One word at a time so I can feel my errorless path.
But guess what?
I miss turning the page.
Now there's no variety,
just another blank white space.
I can't write poetry on this paper…
Someone please help!

SURF NOT TURF

Bruce and I keep a dinghy, down by the dock.
We row out to the skiff, gas up, load the bait
and look for lobsters.

The sky is red and the boat covered with dew.
Egrets are making their rounds. The morning
is so still. Starting up the engine sounds like a shout.
With the sun coming up, we get a whiff
of thawing pogy in the bucket.

We are summer folk in this little town of Maine.
None of us really understands lobsters.
We can only hope they wander
into our traps for tonight's dinner.

When we pull up the lines,
more often than not, they are empty.
Who cares?
We can always tell a story
of that big lobster that got away.

THE THIRD VOLCANO

My name is Tony. I was on the run for twelve long years. Flying back to Hilo in Hawaii

was tough for me. I rented a car at the airport. Everything looked decayed and deserted.

I stopped for beer and headed for the Hawaii National Park. Morris greeted me warmly

at the blue house. He asked me why I never called. I couldn't answer. I told him

I was too exhausted and had to sleep.

Late that night, in the blue house, alone in bed, the past engulfed me.

The same nightmare all over again. Red fire touching the tops of trees, too quick, too quick

…a large blanket of smoke…bubbling molten lava…my girl friend…Denise…holding my hand…

Morris screaming…the cone of the volcano spitting flames and ashes…

we started running

towards a long plateau…and suddenly I was alone.

Where was Denise? I woke in a sweat.

Distraught, I slowly made my way to the kitchen; Morris walked in to start the coffee.

He felt my anxiety. Morris put his hands on my shoulders.

"Let the nightmare be over Tony. Today will be a new beginning."

"But I never found Denise, Morris."

"She'll show up one day, just like you did."

JUST A WORLD WITHOUT WORDS

    It all began
        just like that
    a discovery
        of a world
    without words.
        I never said
    anything; I didn't
        have to; it was the eyes
    of the mermaid on
        the prow of the boat
    and the sounds
        of the ship's foghorn.

TWO POETS IN THE FOG

We are walking together
        under the bridge
        in fog;
I read a poem
        and she reads
        one to me.
Laughter;
        a mystery
        from dense air.
We stop;
        we feel the river;
        we hear its words.
Now we flow
        without bodies,
        without memories.
Where does this bridge take us? To Rumi, the Sufi?
        To narrow streets
        where he once lived?
Does it take us to another country?
        To a door
        where we knock?
The scent of herbs and spices is there, always,
        but he doesn't always answer
        and we have no key.

UNTIL

Silence is there   among doors and windows. . .
moonlight too.   this sad story
   permeates everything
   never leaves
until sleep comes. . .

THREE WOMEN

Three women sit in my
kitchen, talking and laughing
about life and men.
They drink my coffee
and eat my buttered rolls.
I sit by the window
wondering what
they really want,
these three sisters.
I see the children
coming home from school
and hear the names of men.
Suddenly, the women start laughing
at the stupidity of males.
They are feeding my cold, spoiling me
with their food, having so much fun
and I'm happy to have their company.
One is really pretty. I feel better.
Who knows? I offer them wine.
More giggles. Maybe,
just maybe, I'll get lucky
tonight.

IN MEMORY OF RABINDRANATH TAGORE

India received its honored guest,
when it laid him down to rest.
He did not vanish into the night;
his poems and songs still give us his light.

Nations did not heed his words;
now they have to wait in herds.
War and greed are everywhere;
lands are ruined and nearly bare.

In every face
there is no grace.
Each and every country's lie
stays frozen in our eye.

We should follow Tagore in this dark night,
read his poems and experience delight.
Let's sing his songs with a hearty voice,
banishing all fears AND REJOICE!

KIRSTEN

Walking along the beach,
she sees the boat is within her reach
and so she goes to be alone
discarding her phone for peace.

Viking blood demands
she go beyond the bonds of safety;
once there she breathes deeply again
and finds herself.

At dusk she returns home
giving light to the candles that burn,
spreading joy throughout the house.
Her singing brings delight to everyone.

The salmon and rhubarb come out;
laughter and light are about.
Stories of carrying Jack on her back,
and jumping in blue water where jellyfish thrive,

make all feel alive.

HOVERING

The darkness suffocates me
stretching like a python that never ends;
it will swallow me; have I been abandoned?
Everything is going wrong: lost my job,
lost my girl, lost it all.
I feel caged in a mean house
and cannot sing
my songs.

Suddenly, I see a warm light,
but what is it? It swirls around me,
dazzling, getting closer and closer,
an angel hovering above.
Messenger? Hallucination?
Silence, peace and joy,
so very near.

Then gone...morning
waking with sunlight
through the window I'm laughing,
I'm touched...

HOODIE

The image provokes
a flinch away from thought,
a folk demon
or maybe a political symbol.

It never was that way
back in the day.
It was just a cashmere hoodie
in heather gray.
The New York Jets
wore them.

Now there's a theater of the hood
framing a look
or masking headphones.
Music groups use it
to abduct
the listener…

MOHONK

She is always the first
to wake up.
She stands by the window
and sings in the cool dawn light,
unaware.
Her song wakes him and he smiles
as he watches her from their bed.
They have been together
for ten years now.
At first it was her beauty
then came the laughter.
She has such a generosity of spirit,
a love of life that speaks to him.
This morning they walk on Huguenot Drive
up to the pond,
and watch frolicking frogs
near the white lily pads.
He tries to imagine the world
without her.

COME TO ME

Come to me my lovely;
    put your gentle arms
        around me;
shower me
    with your sweet
        love.

It's dark now;
    I can hear your steps.
        I see the candle burning.
"Is that you,
    my beloved?" I cry.
        "Come
this way.
    Heal
        the emptiness I feel."

THE TRAIN STATION

At the station...
snow and wind
rushed towards you
slowly you drew deep breaths
in the snowy, frosty air.
I watched you looking for me.
Stunning and dazzling crystals
floated above you falling along the lighted station.
A blistering storm came rushing between the wheels of the train...
you looked so snug in your red velvet coat. People were rushing
all around you to board the train. You turned and saw me...
tears filled your eyes.
"Where are you going," I yelled.
Wind circled around you
and softened the sound of the whistle.
"All aboard," is all I heard.
Slowly you stepped on the train...
"Stay with me," I cried as the train pulled out.
"Why are you always leaving?" I yelled.
Suddenly, I woke up; it was a dream.
I'm forever running after you even in my sleep.
This need to have you always by my side
never goes away.

THE POSTCARD

The postcard said,
"Meet me in St. Louis
at the Bellevue Hotel at six pm."
Saturday, I packed my suitcase
and arrived early. I waited in the lobby.
Images of her flooded my mind:
walks on the beach at dawn,
nights in bed,
running in the rain,
kissing,
meeting in mysterious places.
At six on the dot, in a cold sweat, I went to the desk
and asked for Sarah Cole.
"I'm sorry, sir, your party has checked out."
"Could you please look again and make sure," I asked.
The clerk looked sad when she returned. "I'm sorry."
I asked if there was a message.
"There is no message from a Ms. Sarah Cole
and none from the other party either."
That's when I knew.
She got her revenge.

THE CHARMER

Sarah places her diaries on her bed in the darkened room
and removes her clothes.
Her long strawberry hair covers her lovely body.
You watch without words.
Once before, she was your lover.
A breeze from the window carries a scent of jasmine.
Sarah lights the colorful beaded lamp by her night table
and begins to read her diaries.
Her sweet voice caresses the words like pressed roses.
She tells the story of youth when her hair flowed wild.
You follow the words mesmerized by her voice.
You are lost.
She has charmed you,
beguiled you,
brought you into her domain
with a web of words.
She has taken over.
You are slipping into her spell.

DARK CITY IN THE SAND

I walk away from the
    city's center,
entering a place where
    tourists are not welcome;
tonight I'll listen
    to the stories of old men
that feature demons and spirits.
    They'll tell me of bleached bones
and ghosts;
    meanwhile,
winds rise
    stars emerge,
leaving images
    on ancient walls.
Music and dance
    will take me away.
No longer will
    I hear your voice again;
no longer. . .

TIBIDABO IN BARCELONA

If not for the rail, my
    body would fail and
sail through the air off this
    high, sacred place.
This past week
    each and every night,
I have tossed and turned
    in my solitary bed
and dreamt of her.
    She came into my life,
when we were young;
    we would play in the
house above the sands.
    Now she's gone.
I stagger backwards
    with nothing to hold on to. . .

ACKNOWLEGEMENT

Without
your touch
Sigrid
there would never
have been
a poem…